We all know that house in the middle of town, where

the grass is dry and the weeds are tall.

the flowers don't grow or blossom at all.

And we all know those people in the middle of our lives

whose hearts are tired. and spirits are sore;

they cannot find joy or hope anymore.

In Mark 12:31, Jesus tells us to love our neighbors as ourselves. When we show love to our neighbors, even in simple ways, we are honoring and obeying God while being a blessing to our neighbors. Young children love to help——it makes them feel useful and important. And helping others is a way to teach children how to put into action the life and love that God has given them. Include your child whenever possible in activities that can

put joy in a heart and a smile on a face.

and make someone glad to know Jesus' grace

. . . maybe even at the house in the middle of your town.

Crystal Bowman

To my dear father-in-law, Robert Bowman Sr.,

and in loving memory of my dear father, Harold Langejans.

—C. B.

To my friends in Garden Grove, California,

who gave so much to me and mine when we needed it.

—J. A.

Published by Standard Publishing, Cincinnati, Ohio
www.standardpub.com

Text Copyright © 2007 by Crystal Bowman
Illustrations Copyright © 2007 by Joy Allen

Printed in: China
Project editor: Laura Derico
Cover & interior design: Wes Youssi, The DesignWorks Group

ISBN 978-0-7847-2098-1

13 12 11 10 09 08   9 8 7 6 5 4 3 2

Library of Congress Control Number: 2007006023

The House in the Middle of Town

Written by
Crystal Bowman

Illustrated by
Joy Allen

Standard PUBLISHING
Bringing The Word to Life

Cincinnati, Ohio

This is the H°uSe in the middle of town;

The shutters are crooked and falling down.

The grass is dry and the weeds are tall,

The flowers don't grow or blossom at all.

This is the GraNdMa with silver hair,

Who rocks all day in her rocking chair.

Her feet are tired, her hands are sore;

She cannot work or clean anymore,

At the house in the middle of town.

This is the Sun that shone in the sky

The day that my neighbors and I came by

With ladders and paint and hammers and nails,

With flowers and rakes and brushes and pails,

At the house in the middle of town.

This is the Cap I decided to wear

To keep the paint drips out of my hair.

I wore my jeans that were faded and worn;

It didn't matter that they were torn,

At the house in the middle of town.

This is the fENCE with cracks and splinters,

Weathered and dry from too many winters.

We patched and painted and polished it too,

Until all the pickets looked shiny and new,

At the house in the middle of town.

This is the Hammer and these are the Nails

That pounded the steps and put up the rails.

We straightened the shutters and oiled the door,

We fastened the boards that were loose on the floor,

At the house in the middle of town.

This is the Brush that helped me scrub

The bathroom floor, the sink, and the tub.

I wiped the windows and cleaned the mirror,

And watched all the fingerprints disappear,

At the house in the middle of town.

This is the pitcher of cool lemonade

We passed around as we sat in the shade,

Talking and laughing, enjoying a break,

Till somebody hollered, "It's time to rake!"

At the house in the middle of town.

This is the Rake I scraped through the grass

To pick up the sticks, the leaves, and the trash.

A truck stopped by to pick up the load,

Piled up high by the side of the road,

At the house in the middle of town.

This is the mailbox, dented and rusty;

The flag is stuck, the inside is musty.

We bought a new box at the hardware store

To replace the one that was there before,

At the house in the middle of town.

These are the flowers we planted outside,

Three rows deep and eleven rows wide.

We pulled the weeds and watered the ground;

We trimmed the bushes that grew all around,

At the house in the middle of town.

This is the Birdhouse we screwed to a pole;
We glued on the roof and carved out a hole.
We sprinkled the floor with grain and seed
So robins would come to sing and feed,
At the house in the middle of town.

These are my Neighbors who worked very hard

To fix up the house and clean up the yard.

Tired and dirty, we're glad that we came

To help out a grandma in Jesus' name,

At the house in the middle of town.

This is the GraNdma with silver hair,

Who rocks all day in her rocking chair.

With joy in her heart and a smile on her face,

She welcomes us all to her beautiful place,

At the house in the middle of town.

CRYSTAL BOWMAN is an accomplished speaker and author of over forty children's books, as well as three books for women. She has written several books in the Little Blessings Series including *Is God Always with Me?* and *Devotions for Preschoolers* (Tyndale). Her holiday board book series (Zonderkidz) includes such titles as *Jesus, Me, and My Christmas Tree, J is for Jesus, My Valentine Story,* and *An Easter Gift for Me*. She is also known for her books of children's poetry—*Cracks in the Sidewalk* and *If Peas Could Taste Like Candy*—and enjoys teaching kids how to write poems. Crystal is involved with MOPS (Mothers of Preschoolers) and Hearts at Home, and is a frequent guest on Christian radio programs. With a background in early childhood education and as a mother of three grown children, she's in tune with what children love to read and what parents want in quality children's literature. Crystal and her husband live in Palm Beach Gardens, Florida, and in Grand Rapids, Michigan.

JOY ALLEN began her art career as a child, winning her first art contest in second grade. In 1997, after a long career in graphic design, she began illustrating picture books. Joy's unique and appealing style helped her gain immediate acceptance in the highly competitive children's book market, with over forty publications in a wide variety of outlets. Some of Joy's recent picture books include: *Being Friends* (Dial), Bank Street book choice; *Mud Pie Annie* (Zonderkidz), Silver Angel Award book; and *The Book of Boys (for Girls)* & *The Book of Girls (for Boys)* (Little, Brown). She is currently illustrator for the *Cam Jansen* mystery books series (Puffin). The grandmother of four, Joy considers her children the best of her creations! She resides in Cameron Park, California.